Latin Favorites
for Accordion

ISBN 978-0-634-05305-4

HAL•LEONARD®
CORPORATION
7777 W. BLUEMOUND RD. P.O. BOX 13819 MILWAUKEE, WI 53213

For all works contained herein:
Unauthorized copying, arranging, adapting, recording or public performance is an infringement of copyright.
Infringers are liable under the law.

Visit Hal Leonard Online at
www.halleonard.com

AMOR
(Amor, Amor, Amor)

Music by GABRIEL RUIZ
Spanish Words by RICARDO LOPEZ MENDEZ
English Words by NORMAN NEWELL

Copyright © 1941, 1943 by Promotora Hispano Americana de Musica, S.A.
Copyrights Renewed
All Rights Administered by Peer International Corporation
International Copyright Secured   All Rights Reserved

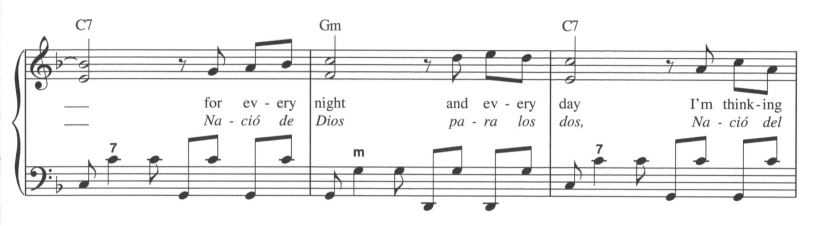

for ev - ery night and ev - ery day, I'm think-ing
Na - ció de Dios para los dos, Na - ció del

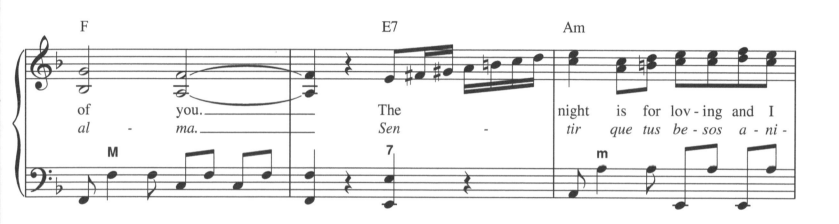

of you._____ The night is for lov - ing and I
al - ma._____ Sen - tir que tus be - sos a - ni -

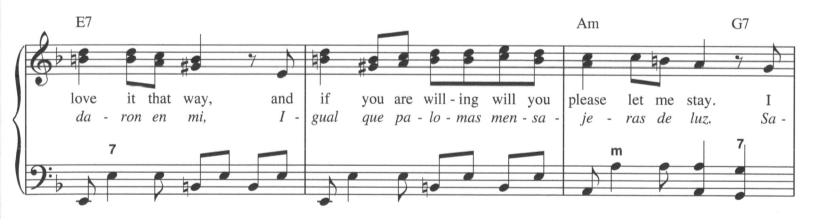

love it that way, and if you are will - ing will you please let me stay. I
da - ron en mi, I - gual que pa - lo - mas men - sa - je - ras de luz. Sa -

can't go on liv - ing if you turn me a - way, so why not give in and let the
ber que mis be - sos se que - da - ron en ti, ha - cien - do en tus la - bios la se -

4

AQUELLOS OJOS VERDES
(Green Eyes)

Music by NILO MENENDEZ
Spanish Words by ADOLFO UTRERA
English Words by E. RIVERA and E. WOODS

Copyright © 1929, 1931 by Peer International Corporation
Copyrights Renewed
International Copyright Secured   All Rights Reserved

our lips meet and our | hearts too, | with a thrill so sub-
de to-das las dul- | *zu - ras* | *que sa-bi - an brin-*

lime. | Those cool and lim-pid | green eyes
dar. | *A - que-llos o - jos* | *ver - des*

a pool where in my | love lies | so deep that in my
se - re - nos co-mo un | *la - go* | *en cu - yas quie - tas*

search - ing | for hap-pi - ness I
a - guas | *un di - a me mi-*

THE BREEZE AND I

Words by AL STILLMAN
Music by ERNESTO LECUONA

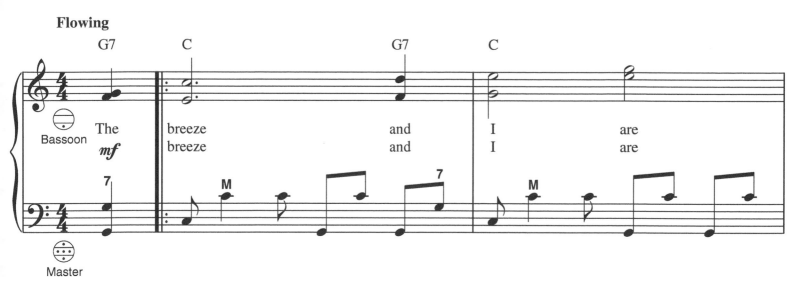

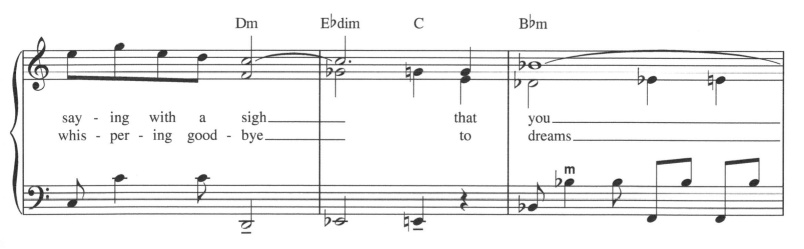

Copyright © 1928 by Edward B. Marks Music Company
Copyright Renewed
International Copyright Secured   All Rights Reserved
Used by Permission

10

11

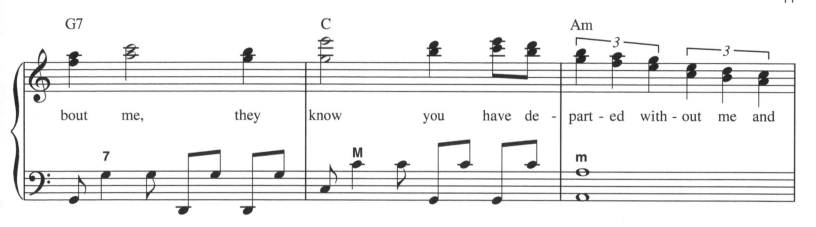

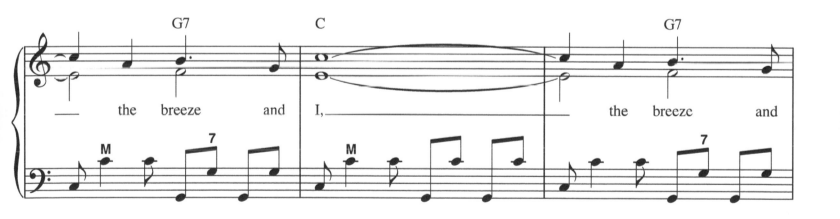

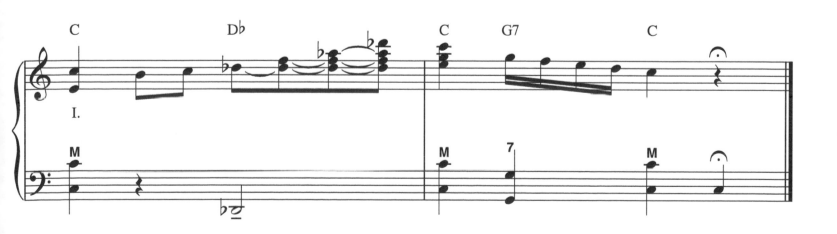

BÉSAME MUCHO
(Kiss Me Much)

Music and Spanish Words by CONSUELO VELAZQUEZ
English Words by SUNNY SKYLAR

Bé - sa - me,_____ bé - sa - me
Bé - sa - me,_____ bé - sa - me

mu - cho,_____ each time I cling to your
mu - cho,_____ co - mo si fue - ra es - ta

kiss I hear mu - sic di - vine.
no - che la úl - ti - ma vez;

Copyright © 1941, 1943 by Promotora Hispano Americana de Musica, S.A.
Copyrights Renewed
All Rights Administered by Peer International Corporation
International Copyright Secured   All Rights Reserved

14

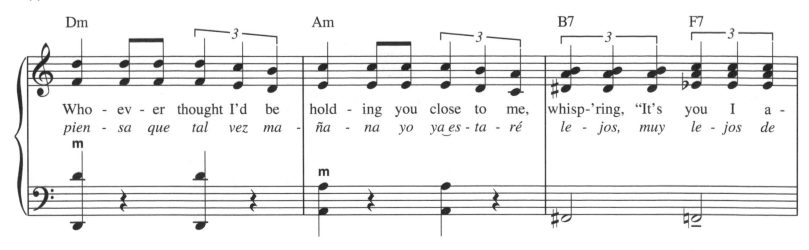

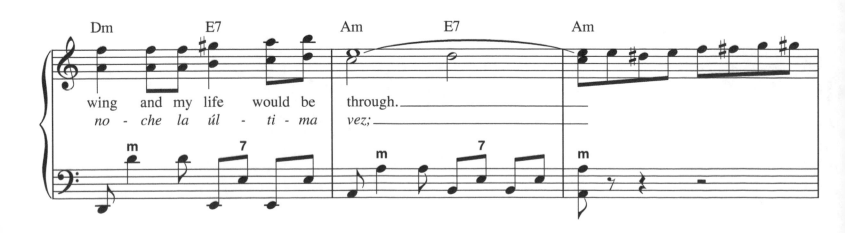

FLAMINGO

Lyric by ED ANDERSON
Music by TED GROUYA

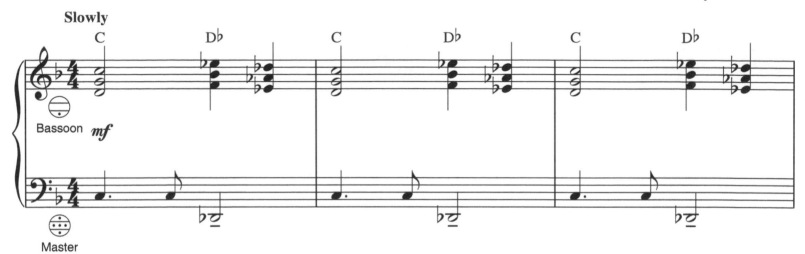

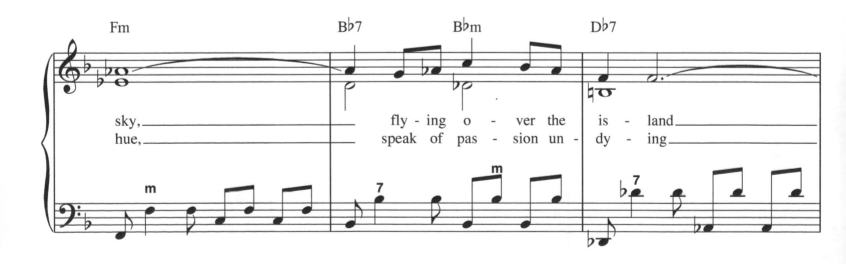

© 1941 TEMPO MUSIC, INC.
© Renewed EDWIN H. MORRIS & COMPANY, A Division of MPL Communications, Inc. and GROUYA PUBLISHING
All Rights for GROUYA PUBLISHING Administered by THE SONGWRITERS GUILD OF AMERICA
All Rights Reserved

18

HOW INSENSITIVE
(Insensatez)

Music by ANTONIO CARLOS JOBIM
Original Words by VINICIUS DE MORAES
English Words by NORMAN GIMBEL

Copyright © 1963, 1964 ANTONIO CARLOS JOBIM and VINICIUS DE MORAES, Brazil
Copyright Renewed and Assigned to UNIVERSAL - DUCHESS MUSIC CORPORATION and NEW THUNDER MUSIC, INC.
All Rights for NEW THUNDER MUSIC, INC. Administered by GIMBEL MUSIC GROUP, INC. (P.O. Box 15221, Beverly Hills, CA 90209 USA)
All Rights Reserved   Used by Permission

THE GIRL FROM IPANEMA
(Garôta de Ipanema)

Music by ANTONIO CARLOS JOBIM
English Words by NORMAN GIMBEL
Original Words by VINICIUS DE MORAES

Copyright © 1963 ANTONIO CARLOS JOBIM and VINICIUS DE MORAES, BRAZIL
Copyright Renewed and Assigned to UNIVERSAL - DUCHESS MUSIC CORPORATION and NEW THUNDER MUSIC, INC.
All Rights for NEW THUNDER MUSIC, INC. Administered by GIMBEL MUSIC GROUP, INC. (P.O. Box 15221, Beverly Hills, CA 90209 USA)
All Rights Reserved   Used by Permission

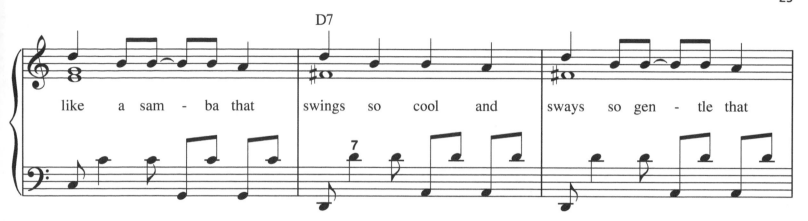

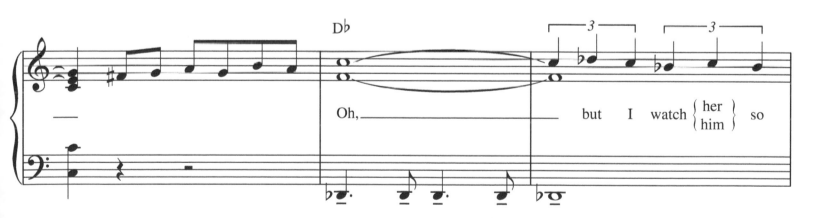

24

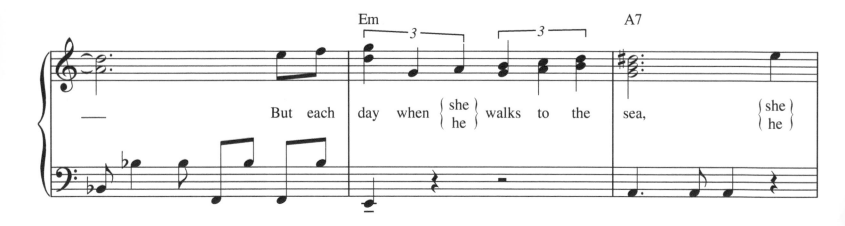

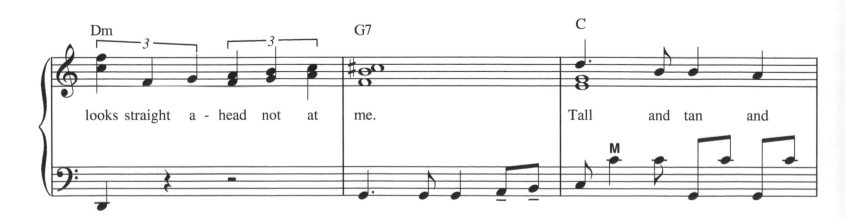

MAMBO JAMBO
(Que Rico el Mambo)

English Words by RAYMOND KARL
and CHARLIE TOWNE
Original Words and Music by DAMASO PEREZ PRADO

Fast Latin

Copyright © 1950 by Peer International Corporation
Copyright Renewed
International Copyright Secured   All Rights Reserved

she'll be re - luc - tant to say "a - di - os." ___ Dif - f'rent from
here is the part where she'll want to be kissed. ___

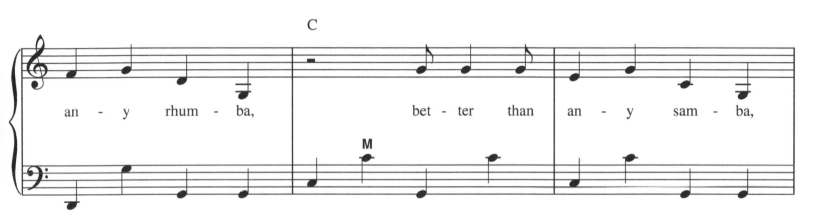

an - y rhum - ba, better than an - y sam - ba,

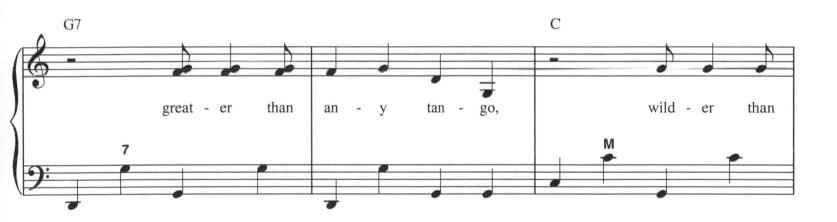

great - er than an - y tan - go, wild - er than

an - y con - ga. The min - ute that you be - gin, ___
You'll find at the break of day, ___

28

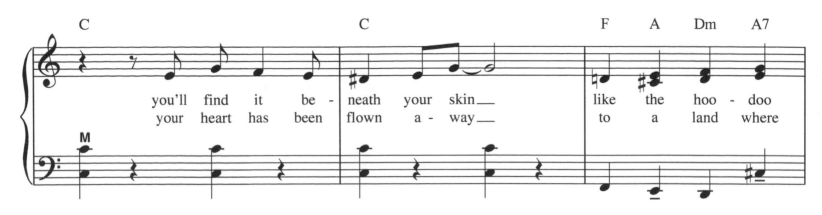

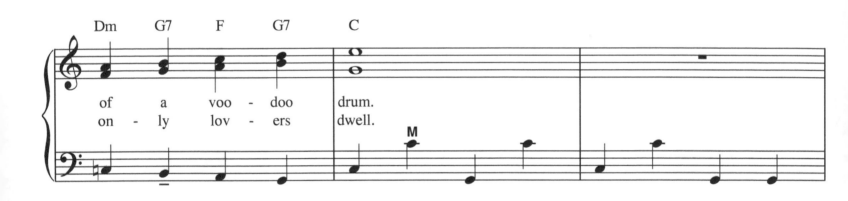

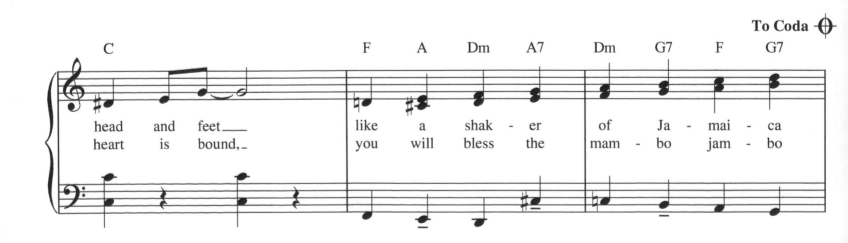

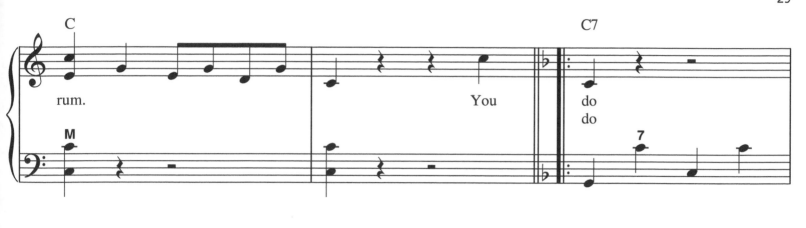

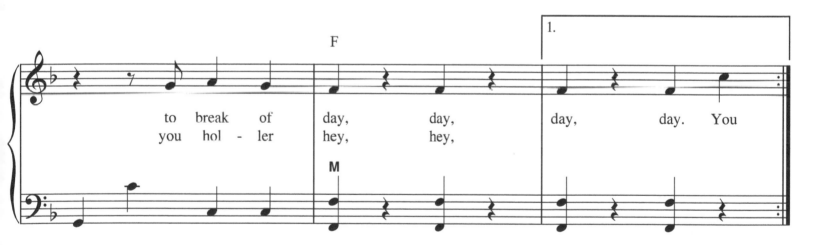

MEDITATION
(Meditacáo)

Music by ANTONIO CARLOS JOBIM
Original Words by NEWTON MENDONCA
English Words by NORMAN GIMBEL

Relaxed Bossa Nova

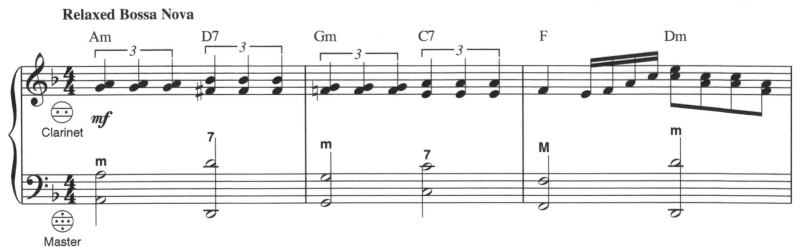

Copyright © 1962, 1965 ANTONIO CARLOS JOBIM and MRS. NEWTON MENDONCA, BRAZIL
Copyright Renewed and Assigned to UNIVERSAL - DUCHESS MUSIC CORPORATION and NEW THUNDER MUSIC, INC.
All Rights for NEW THUNDER MUSIC, INC. Administered by GIMBEL MUSIC GROUP, INC. (P.O. Box 15221, Beverly Hills, CA 90209 USA)
All Rights Reserved   Used by Permission

Yes,_____ I love you so_____

and that for me___ is all I need___ to

know._____ I_____

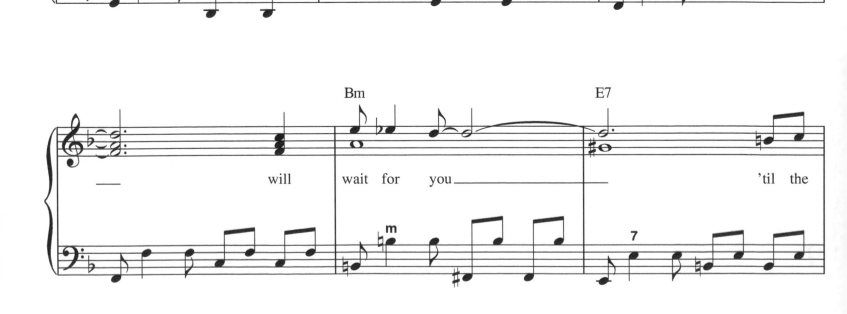

___ will wait for you_____ 'til the

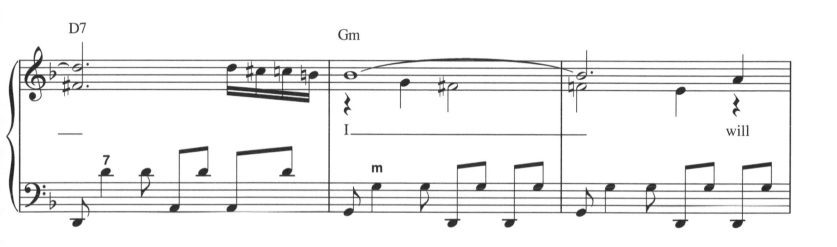

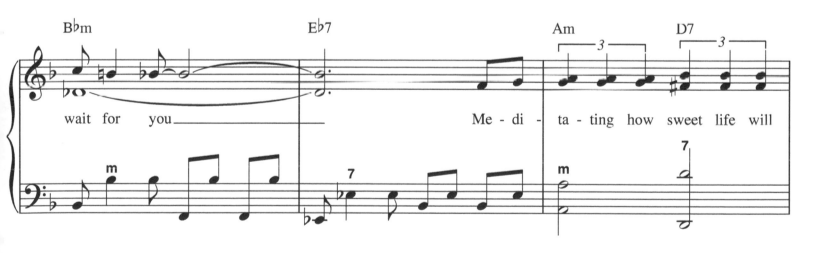

MIAMI BEACH RUMBA

Words by ALBERT GAMSE
Music by IRVING FIELDS

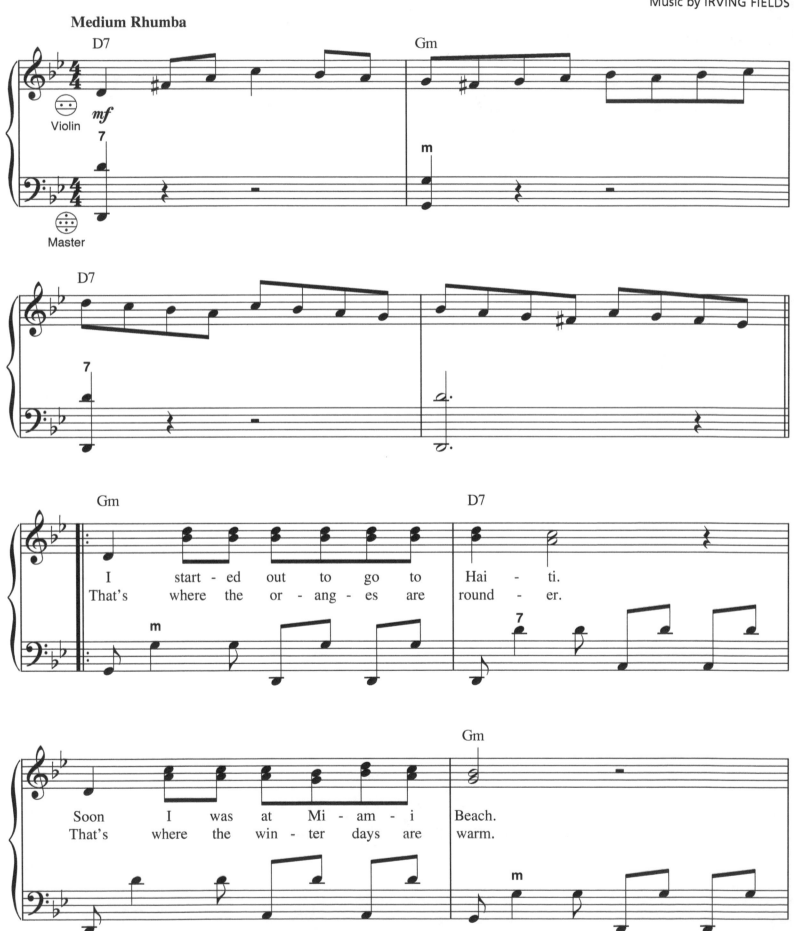

Copyright © 1946, 1962 by Edward B. Marks Music Company
Copyrights Renewed
International Copyright Secured   All Rights Reserved
Used by Permission

36

fair. The temp-'ra-ture was o - ver eight - y, which

they call cool down there! I did - n't go where I in -

tend - ed, far great - er joy was in my reach.

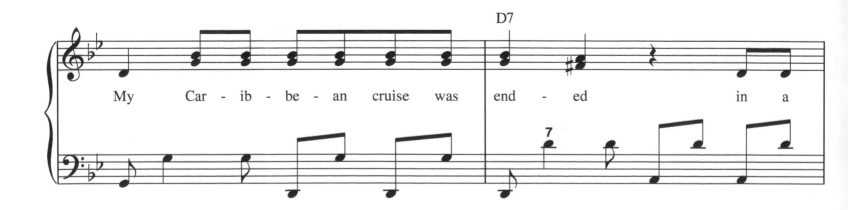

My Car - ib - be - an cruise was end - ed in a

ONLY ONCE IN MY LIFE
(Solamente Una Vez)

Music and Spanish Words by AGUSTIN LARA
English Words by RICK CARNES and JANIS CARNES

Copyright © 1998 by Songs Of Peer, Ltd.
International Copyright Secured   All Rights Reserved

39

40

PERFIDIA

Words and Music by
ALBERTO DOMINGUEZ

Copyright © 1939 by Peer International Corporation
Copyright Renewed
International Copyright Secured   All Rights Reserved

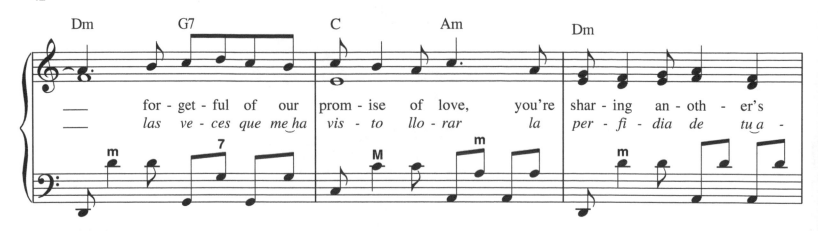

for - get - ful of our prom - ise of love, you're shar - ing an - oth - er's
las ve - ces que me ha vis - to llo - rar la per - fi - dia de tu a -

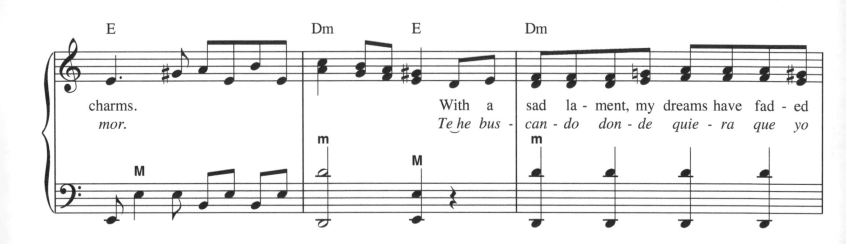

charms.
mor.

With a sad la - ment, my dreams have fad - ed
Te he bus - can - do don - de quie - ra que yo

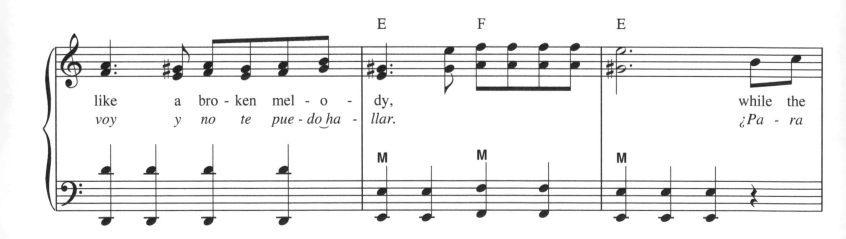

like a bro - ken mel - o - dy,
voy y no te pue - do ha - llar.

while the
¿Pa - ra

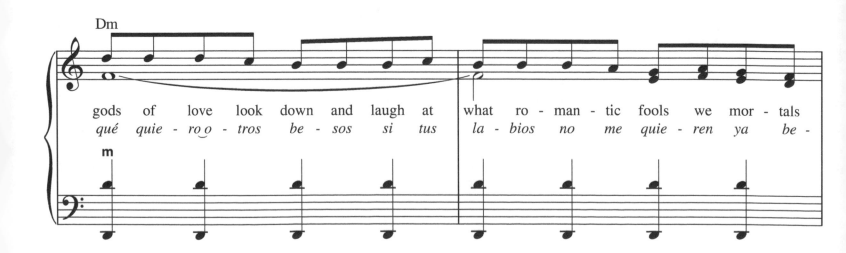

gods of love look down and laugh at what ro - man - tic fools we mor - tals
qué quie - ro o - tros be - sos si tus la - bios no me quie - ren ya be -

QUIZÁS, QUIZÁS, QUIZÁS
(Perhaps, Perhaps, Perhaps)

Music and Spanish Words by OSVALDO FARRES
English Words by JOE DAVIS

Copyright © 1947 by Southern Music Pub. Co. Inc.
Copyright Renewed
International Copyright Secured All Rights Reserved

46

SPANISH EYES

Words by CHARLES SINGLETON and EDDIE SNYDER
Music by BERT KAEMPFERT

© 1965, 1966 (Renewed 1993, 1994) EDITION DOMA BERT KAEMPFERT
All Rights for the world, excluding Germany, Austria and Switzerland, Controlled and Administered by SCREEN GEMS-EMI MUSIC INC.
All Rights Reserved   International Copyright Secured   Used by Permission

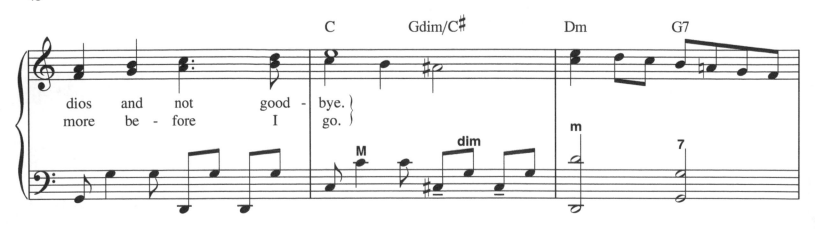

dios   and   not   good - bye.
more   be - fore   I   go.

Soon_____   I'll   re - turn,_____

bring - ing   you all   the   love   your   heart can   hold._____

_____   Please_____   say   Sí

POINCIANA
(Song of the Tree)

Words by BUDDY BERNIER
Music by NAT SIMON

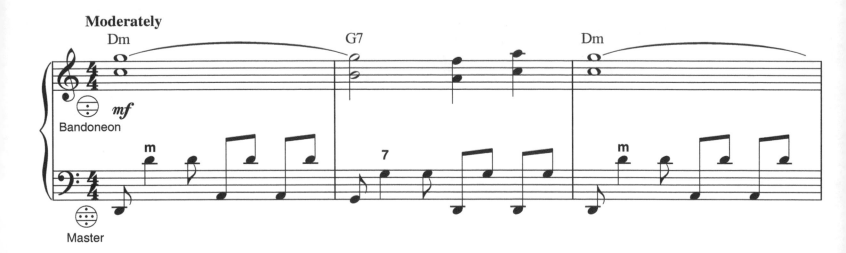

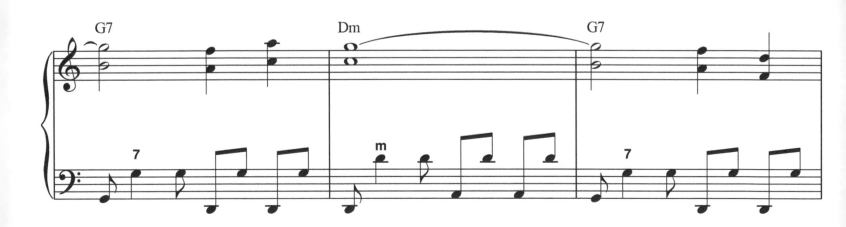

Copyright © 1936 by Chappell & Co.
Copyright Renewed
International Copyright Secured   All Rights Reserved

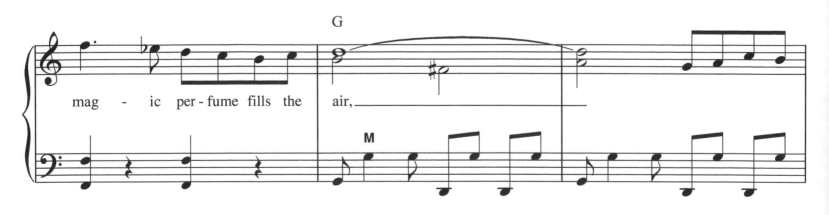

mag - ic per - fume fills the air,_____

to and fro you sway, my heart's in time, I've learned to care._____

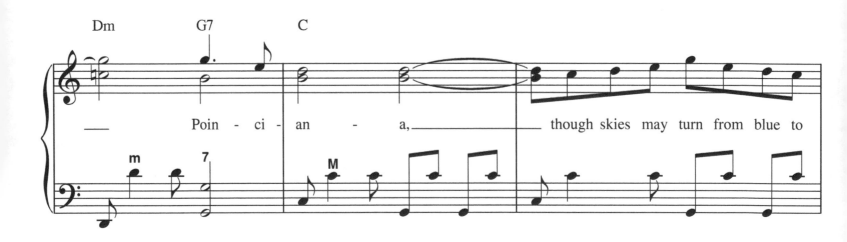

___ Poin - ci - an - a,_____ though skies may turn from blue to

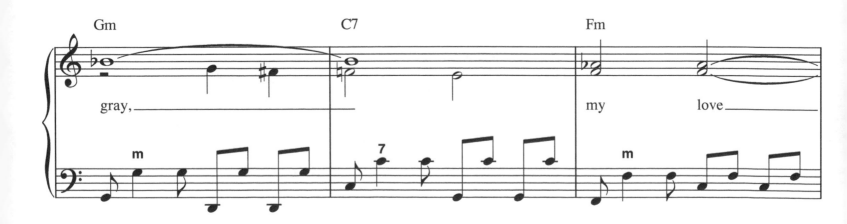

gray,_____ my love_____ to

will live for - ev - er and a day.

SO NICE
(Summer Samba)

Original Words and Music by MARCOS VALLE
and PAULO SERGIO VALLE
English Words by NORMAN GIMBEL

Relaxed Bossa Nova

Accordion
mf
Master

Some-one to hold me tight, that would be ver - y nice, some-one to love me right,

that would be ver - y nice. Some-one to un-der-stand each lit-tle dream_ in me,

some-one to take my hand, to be a team_ with me. So nice,_____
m

Copyright © 1965, 1966 MARCOS VALLE and PAULO SERGIO VALLE, BRAZIL
Copyright Renewed and Assigned to UNIVERSAL - MCA MUSIC PUBLISHING, A Division of Universal Studios, Inc. and NEW THUNDER MUSIC, INC.
All Rights for NEW THUNDER MUSIC, INC. Administered by GIMBEL MUSIC GROUP, INC. (P.O. Box 15221, Beverly Hills, CA 90209 USA)
All Rights Reserved   Used by Permission

then give his heart___ to me. Some-one who's read-y to give love a start___ with me.

Oh yes,___ that would be so nice.___

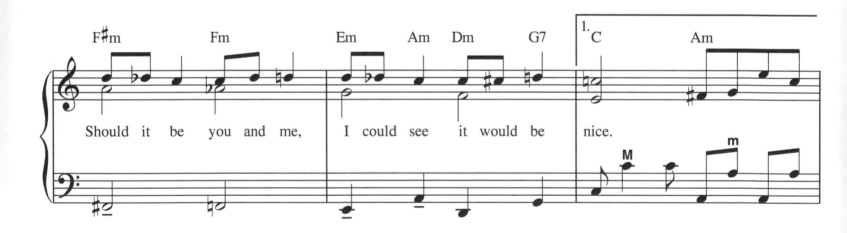

Should it be you and me, I could see it would be nice.

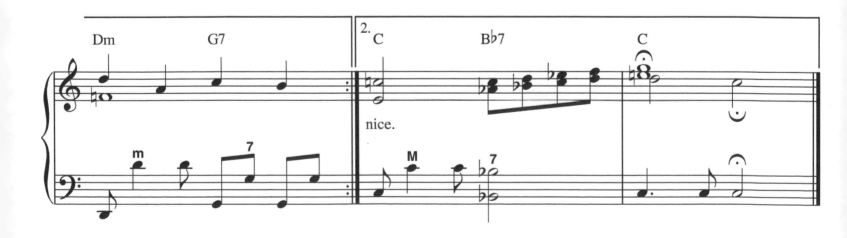

nice.

THIS MASQUERADE

Words and Music by
LEON RUSSELL

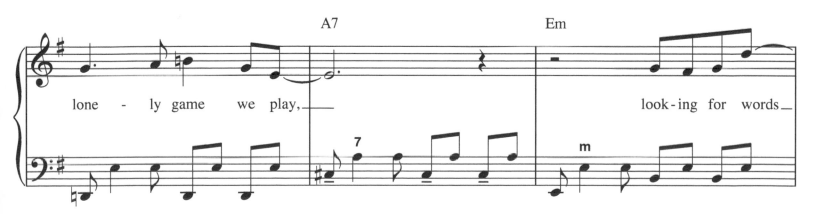

Copyright © 1972, 1973; Renewed 2000, 2001 DreamWorks Music Publishing LLC d/b/a Stuck On Music (BMI) and Embassy Music Corp. (BMI)
Worldwide Rights for DreamWorks Music Publishing LLC d/b/a Stuck On Music Administered by Cherry River Music Co.
International Copyright Secured   All Rights Reserved

58

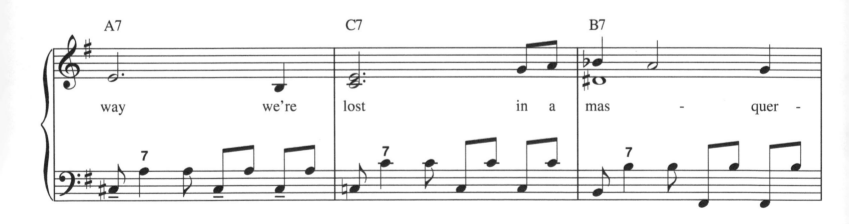

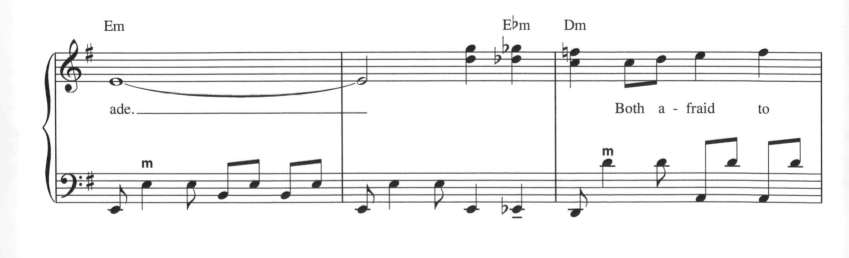

say we're just___ too far a - way__

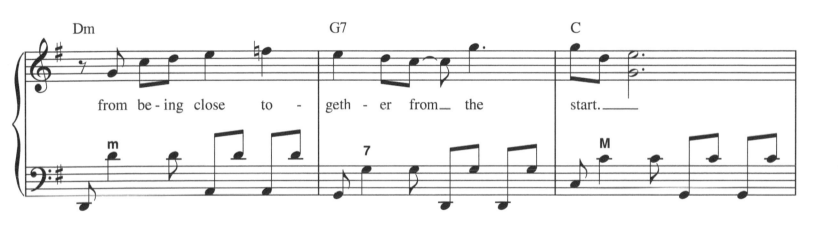

from be - ing close to - geth - er from__ the start._____

We tried to talk__ it o - ver, but the

words got in__ the__ way.__ We're lost in -

60

side   this   lone - ly game___ we play.___

Thoughts of leav - ing   dis - ap - pear___ ev - 'ry time I see   your eyes.___

___   No mat - ter how   hard   I___

try___   to un - der - stand   the

rea - sons that we car - ry on___ this way, we're

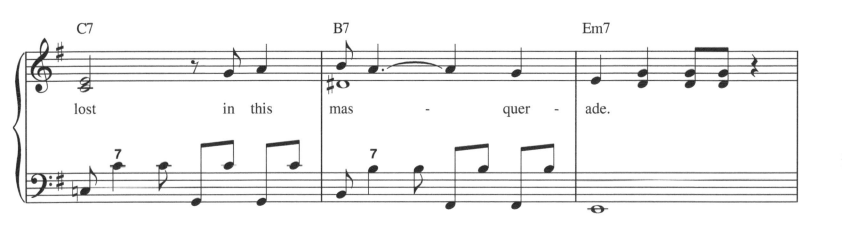

lost in this mas - quer - ade.

SWAY
(Quien Será)

English Words by NORMAN GIMBEL
Spanish Words and Music by PABLO BELTRAN RUIZ

Copyright © 1954 by Peer International Corporation
Copyright Renewed
International Copyright Secured   All Rights Reserved

63

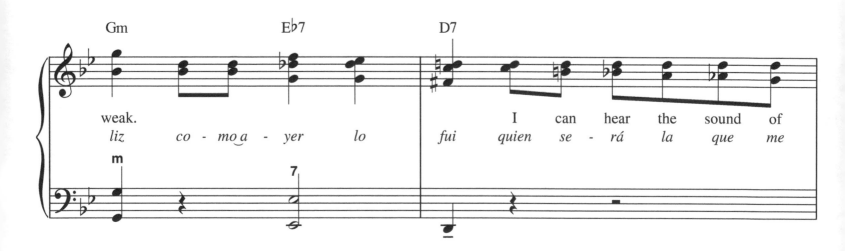

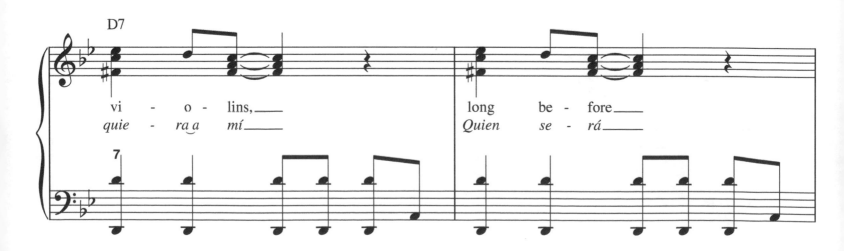

WHAT A DIFF'RENCE A DAY MADE

English Words by STANLEY ADAMS
Music and Spanish Words by MARIA GREVER

Copyright © 1934 by Edward B. Marks Music Company
Copyright Renewed and Assigned to Stanley Adams Music, Inc. and Zomba Golden Sands Inc.
All Rights for Stanley Adams Music, Inc. Administered by The Songwriters Guild Of America
International Copyright Secured   All Rights Reserved
Used by Permission

68

YOURS
(Cuando Se Quiere de Veras)

Words by ALBERT GAMSE and JACK SHERR
Music by GONZALO ROIG

Copyright © 1931, 1937 by Edward B. Marks Music Company
Copyright Renewed
International Copyright Secured   All Rights Reserved
Used by Permission

you, dear,_____ I bring._____

_____ Yours in the gray of De-

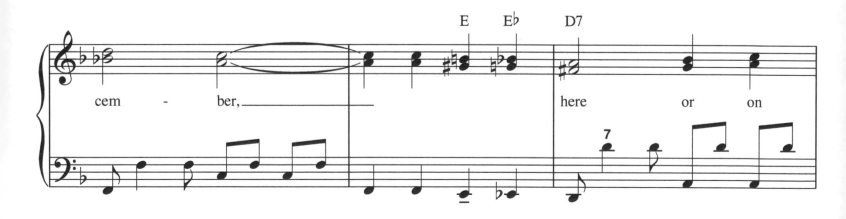

cem - ber,_____ here or on

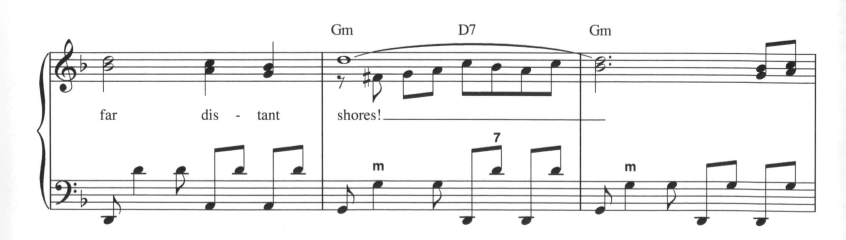

far dis - tant shores!_____

A COLLECTION OF ALL-TIME FAVORITES
FOR ACCORDION

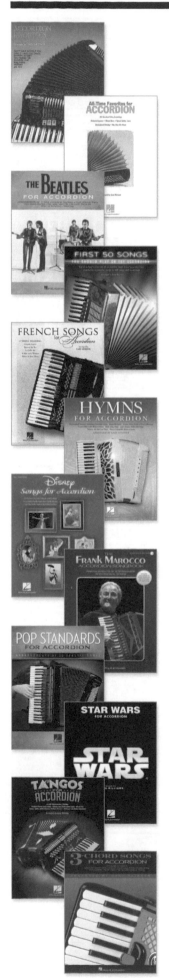

ACCORDION FAVORITES
arr. Gary Meisner

16 all-time favorites, arranged for accordion, including: Can't Smile Without You • Could I Have This Dance • Endless Love • Memory • Sunrise, Sunset • I.O.U. • and more.
00359012.................................$12.99

ALL-TIME FAVORITES FOR ACCORDION
arr. Gary Meisner

20 must-know standards arranged for accordions. Includes: Ain't Misbehavin' • Autumn Leaves • Crazy • Hello, Dolly! • Hey, Good Lookin' • Moon River • Speak Softly, Love • Unchained Melody • The Way We Were • Zip-A-Dee-Doo-Dah • and more.
00311088.................................$12.99

THE BEATLES FOR ACCORDION

17 hits from the Lads from Liverpool have been arranged for accordion. Includes: All You Need Is Love • Eleanor Rigby • The Fool on the Hill • Here Comes the Sun • Hey Jude • In My Life • Let It Be • Ob-La-Di, Ob-La-Da • Penny Lane • When I'm Sixty-Four • Yesterday • and more.
00268724 ....$14.99

BROADWAY FAVORITES
arr. Ken Kotwitz

A collection of 17 wonderful show songs, including: Don't Cry for Me Argentina • Getting to Know You • If I Were a Rich Man • Oklahoma • People Will Say We're in Love • We Kiss in a Shadow.
00490157.................................$10.99

DISNEY SONGS FOR ACCORDION – 3RD EDITION

13 Disney favorites especially arranged for accordion, including: Be Our Guest • Beauty and the Beast • Can You Feel the Love Tonight • Chim Chim Cher-ee • It's a Small World • Let It Go • Under the Sea • A Whole New World • You'll Be in My Heart • Zip-A-Dee-Doo-Dah • and more!
00152508 ....$12.99

FIRST 50 SONGS YOU SHOULD PLAY ON THE ACCORDION
arr. Gary Meisner

If you're new to the accordion, you are probably eager to learn some songs. This book provides 50 simplified arrangements of must-know popular standards, folk songs and show tunes, including: All of Me • Beer Barrel Polka • Carnival of Venice • Edelweiss • Hava Nagila (Let's Be Happy) • Hernando's Hideaway • Jambalaya (On the Bayou) • Lady of Spain • Moon River • 'O Sole Mio • Sentimental Journey • Somewhere, My Love • That's Amore (That's Love) • Under Paris Skies • and more. Includes lyrics when applicable.
00250269 ....$16.99

FRENCH SONGS FOR ACCORDION
arr. Gary Meisner

A très magnifique collection of 17 French standards arranged for the accordion. Includes: Autumn Leaves • Beyond the Sea • C'est Magnifique • I Love Paris • La Marseillaise • Let It Be Me (Je T'appartiens) • Under Paris Skies • Watch What Happens • and more.
00311498.................................$10.99

HYMNS FOR ACCORDION
arr. Gary Meisner

24 treasured sacred favorites arranged for accordion, including: Amazing Grace • Beautiful Savior • Come, Thou Fount of Every Blessing • Crown Him with Many Crowns • Holy, Holy, Holy • It Is Well with My Soul • Just a Closer Walk with Thee • A Mighty Fortress Is Our God • Nearer, My God, to Thee • The Old Rugged Cross • Rock of Ages • What a Friend We Have in Jesus • and more.
00277160 ....$9.99

ITALIAN SONGS FOR ACCORDION
arr. Gary Meisner

17 favorite Italian standards arranged for accordion, including: Carnival of Venice • Ciribiribin • Come Back to Sorrento • Funiculi, Funicula • La donna è mobile • La Spagnola • 'O Sole Mio • Santa Lucia • Tarantella • and more.
00311089.................................$9.95

LATIN FAVORITES FOR ACCORDION
arr. Gary Meisner

20 Latin favorites, including: Bésame Mucho (Kiss Me Much) • The Girl from Ipanema • How Insensitive (Insensatez) • Perfidia • Spanish Eyes • So Nice (Summer Samba) • and more.
00310932.................................$14.99

THE FRANK MAROCCO ACCORDION SONGBOOK

This songbook includes arrangements and recordings of 15 standards and original songs from legendary jazz accordionist Frank Marocco, including: All the Things You Are • Autumn Leaves • Beyond the Sea • Moon River • Moonlight in Vermont • Stormy Weather (Keeps Rainin' All the Time) • and more!
00233441 Book/Online Audio...............$19.99

POP STANDARDS FOR ACCORDION
Arrangements of 20 Classic Songs

20 classic pop standards arranged for accordion are included in this collection: Annie's Song • Chances Are • For Once in My Life • Help Me Make It Through the Night • My Cherie Amour • Ramblin' Rose • (Sittin' On) The Dock of the Bay • That's Amore (That's Love) • Unchained Melody • and more.
00254822 ....$14.99

POLKA FAVORITES
arr. Kenny Kotwitz

An exciting new collection of 16 songs, including: Beer Barrel Polka • Liechtensteiner Polka • My Melody of Love • Paloma Blanca • Pennsylvania Polka • Too Fat Polka • and more.
00311573.................................$12.99

STAR WARS FOR ACCORDION

A dozen songs from the Star Wars franchise: The Imperial March (Darth Vader's Theme) • Luke and Leia • March of the Resistance • Princess Leia's Theme • Rey's Theme • Star Wars (Main Theme) • and more.
00157380 ....$14.99

TANGOS FOR ACCORDION
arr. Gary Meisner

Every accordionist needs to know some tangos! Here are 15 favorites: Amapola (Pretty Little Poppy) • Aquellos Ojos Verdes (Green Eyes) • Hernando's Hideaway • Jalousie (Jealousy) • Kiss of Fire • La Cumparsita (The Masked One) • Quizás, Quizás, Quizás (Perhaps, Perhaps, Perhaps) • The Rain in Spain • Tango of Roses • Whatever Lola Wants (Lola Gets) • and more!
00122252 ....$9.99

3-CHORD SONGS FOR ACCORDION
arr. Gary Meisner

Here are nearly 30 songs that are easy to play but still sound great! Includes: Amazing Grace • Can Can • Danny Boy • For He's a Jolly Good Fellow • He's Got the Whole World in His Hands • Just a Closer Walk with Thee • La Paloma Blanca (The White Dove) • My Country, 'Tis of Thee • Ode to Joy • Oh! Susanna • Yankee Doodle • The Yellow Rose of Texas • and more.
00312104 ....$12.99

LAWRENCE WELK'S POLKA FOLIO

More than 50 famous polkas, schottisches and waltzes arranged for piano and accordion, including: Blue Eyes • Budweiser Polka • Clarinet Polka • Cuckoo Polka • The Dove Polka • Draw One Polka • Gypsy Polka • Helena Polka • International Waltzes • Let's Have Another One • Schnitzelbank • Shuffle Schottische • Squeeze Box Polka • Waldteuful Waltzes • and more.
00123218.................................$12.99

Prices, contents & availability subject to change without notice.

Disney artwork & characters ™ & © 2019 Disney

HAL•LEONARD®
Visit Hal Leonard Online at
www.halleonard.com